Everything You Need to Know About

Smoking

Teenagers sometimes start to smoke because they think it will make them look cool.

Everything You Need to Know About
Smoking

Elizabeth Keyishian

Series Editor: Evan Stark, Ph.D.

Rosen Publishing Group, Inc.
New York

Published in 1989, 1993, 1995, 1997, 2000 by The Rosen Publishing Group, Inc.
29 East 21st Street, New York, NY 10010

Revised Edition 2000

Library of Congress Cataloging-in-Publication Data

Keyishian, Elizabeth
    Everything you need to know about smoking/Elizabeth Keyishian
    (The need to know library)
    Includes bibliographical references and index.
    ISBN 0–8239–3221–4
    1. Tobacco habit—Juvenile literature. 2. Smoking—Juvenile literature.
3. Youth—Tobacco use—Juvenile literature. [1. Smoking.] I. Title. II.
Title: Smoking. III. Series.
HV5745.K48 1989
813.85—dc20   89–10256
                                               CIP

                                               AC

Manufactured in the United States of America

Contents

Introduction: The Truth About Smoking

Have you ever heard someone say that she is trying to quit smoking? And when you check back with that person a short time later, she tells you either that she is still struggling to quit or that she just could not do it and has already given up? Smoking is not an easy habit to break. Many smokers wish that they had never started smoking. Perhaps they started because "everyone was doing it" or because they thought it would make them seem cool or more grown-up. Perhaps they just did not know any better.

This book will give you all the information you need to make an educated decision about whether or not you want to smoke. The chances are that once you start smoking cigarettes, cigars, or a pipe, you will become addicted. Addiction makes quitting difficult when you do not want to smoke anymore.

Cigarettes are addictive because they contain nicotine. Nicotine is a powerful and addictive drug. It is what gives you a "buzz," or a high, when you smoke. It hooks you and keeps you coming back for more. Even if someone successfully quits, it is not uncommon for him or her to start smoking again as much as a year or more after the last cigarette. "Once a smoker, always a smoker," says Carol, who has not smoked a cigarette in more than twenty-eight years. "Please don't ask me to hold your cigarette for you," she says, "or I'll start right up again." After all these years, she knows just how addictive cigarettes can be.

Every day about 3,000 teens try their first cigarette. Many eventually become daily smokers. If you ask these teens if they think they will still be smoking in five years, 75 percent of them will say no. They are wrong. According to a study by the Centers for Disease Control, only 13.5 percent successfully stop. Of teens surveyed who tried cigarettes, 36 percent of them gain the habit, the study says.

Teens want to be cool, fit in, and have friends. However, picking up a harmful, potentially lifelong habit does not make a person cool. Think about it. Smoking-related illnesses account for more than 400,000 deaths in the United States every year. They include the following:

- Lung cancer and other smoking-related cancers
- Heart disease
- Stained teeth and bad breath

- Respiratory problems such as coughing and wheezing
- Loss of the ability to smell and taste
- Sexual problems

Since two million smokers either quit or die every year, tobacco companies have to find ways to attract new smokers. They focus on young people, especially teens who are just starting to make choices about their lives. Clever yet deceptive advertising makes smoking seem like a lifestyle choice that is fun, rewarding, and socially acceptable.

However, the advertisements do not tell the whole story. Tobacco companies are now paying a price for not revealing the health risks associated with smoking. Across the country, they are being sued for millions of dollars by smokers who are suffering smoking-related health problems and by the families of people who have died from smoking-related illnesses.

Now that you have heard some of the facts, do you still think smoking sounds cool? Is smoking really worth the damage it will cause your body? Deciding whether or not to smoke is your choice. But you should be aware of the risks involved. This book will help you understand your options, give you some important facts to think about, and prepare you to make a decision that, in the end, could be a matter of life and death.

Chapter One | Why Start Smoking?

Many young people start smoking because those around them do. Their parents, brothers and sisters, relatives, or friends smoke, so it does not seem like a big deal. In fact, you may even think that you should smoke because others do and you want to be like them. But admiring people you care about does not mean that you should admire smoking.

In the media, smoking is often used as a sign of freedom, rebellion, or being fashionable or hip. It does not appear to be dangerous because so many people seem to be doing it, and there do not seem to be any negative side effects.

In fact, smoking is a big deal. The nicotine in cigarettes has been found to be more addictive than crack cocaine or alcohol. The younger you are when you start, the harder it is to quit as an adult. In other words, you may think that you can smoke a cigarette here and there in social situations, and that's it. It is not that simple, however.

Your body starts to crave nicotine. In one study, 90 percent of young people who tried to stop smoking experienced withdrawal symptoms. Without even knowing it, you can become addicted to smoking just by having an occasional cigarette.

Remember, smoking is not something you have to do. If you never do it, you will never miss it, and you will never experience the pain of addiction. Smoking is not something that you would naturally do—like eating or sleeping—so why even start?

Still, it might be hard if you have friends who start smoking and want you to try it, too. You may feel pressure to light up with your friends so that you can fit in and be part of the group. The main thing to remember, though, is that your body is yours and no one else's. You will suffer the consequences of what smoking does to your body, and you will also be hurting people around you with the secondhand smoke of cigarettes. It is your choice whether to smoke, but know that smoking is not a habit you can easily give up. You will find that standing up to peer pressure is much easier than standing up to nicotine dependence.

Some young people start smoking because they think it makes them look grown-up. Probably not true. Young people smoke because they see older people smoke and want to be treated as an adult. The truth is young

Your first cigarette can make you feel sick.

people who smoke just look as though they are trying to be something they are not. Being adult means acting responsibly, not recklessly—and smoking is reckless to your health and the health of those around you.

You can tell that smoking is bad for you by the way your body reacts to it. The first time you smoke, it usually makes you cough. You may choke or feel dizzy. You may even feel sick enough to throw up. Cigarette smoke contains tar, which stays in your lungs even though you blow the smoke back out through your nose or mouth. Tar in your lungs can cause cancer. Smoking can also cause heart disease and other serious health problems. Even if you do enjoy smoking, is the pleasure worth sacrificing your health or even your life?

Think about all of these things when someone offers you a cigarette or talks about how cool it is to smoke. Do not be afraid to say no. There are no good reasons to start smoking. People will respect you for making your own decision.

Chapter Two | The Health Risks

You probably know that smoking can lead to heart disease and lung cancer. Recently, however, a study was done that determined a link between cigarette smoking and colon cancer. If you start smoking when you are young, the increased risk of colon cancer stays with you even after you quit. In other words, smoking can cause permanent damage.

This is only one of the many discoveries scientists have made about the negative effects of smoking on the human body. It may not seem important now, but you will be taking care of your body for a long time. Why not get a head start?

To understand how terrible smoking is for you, look at what each cigarette contains:

- Nicotine, a habit-forming drug

- Black tars that stick to the lining of your lungs and make it hard to breathe

- Carbon monoxide and chemicals that poison your lungs

Every drag on a cigarette leaves those things in your lungs. In addition, nicotine speeds up your heart and makes your nerves shaky. In large doses, it is poisonous. You quickly become addicted to it.

The tars coat the inside of your lungs and make it hard to breathe. Your heart has to work harder. It is not getting enough oxygen from your stuffed-up lungs. Carbon monoxide prevents oxygen from reaching your heart. That can cause heart disease.

How does smoking affect your body? Your body is like a sensitive machine. Its parts work together to keep you healthy. When you smoke, you damage many parts of the machine, which makes it break down. Soon the machine stops working.

You breathe all day long. You take about 600 million breaths during your lifetime. When was the last time you said, "Wow, I'm breathing." Probably never. You have too many other things to think about. You think about breathing only when it hurts to breathe.

When you smoke, you make breathing more difficult. Try running up a flight of stairs. You might find

Smoking reduces lung power. It becomes difficult to breathe while running or walking.

yourself breathing very heavily, and your heart might race.

There are pictures that can show you what happens to your lungs and heart when you smoke. Surgeons who operate on smokers say that the lungs are black from tar.

The lungs bring oxygen into the body and pump carbon dioxide out. They are made of tubes called bronchi. The tubes lead into tiny balloonlike sacs. In the tubes, tiny hairs (called cilia) brush mucus out of the airways.

Nicotine, the drug in tobacco, paralyzes your cilia. The cilia cannot push the mucus out of the way, so your airways get clogged. Tars and chemicals settle in the airways, and the cilia die. The smoker has to cough to get the mucus out of the lungs. That is known as smoker's cough. It sounds as if the person is choking and wheezing.

The bronchi (those tubes in your lungs) get sore with all that coughing. The smoker then develops chronic bronchitis. It becomes more painful and difficult to breathe.

People with bronchitis often develop emphysema, a disease that makes it hard to breathe. Many of them have to use a wheelchair. Simple movements—like walking and breathing—become hard to perform. You may have seen someone with emphysema. People with emphysema often have to bring a cart carrying a heavy tank of oxygen wherever they go.

People who smoke for a long time may also get cancer. The chemicals and tar in cigarettes can make the body's cells grow out of control. They form lumps, or tumors, in the lungs. The cancerous lumps block breathing.

There is some good news. As soon as you stop smoking, your body begins to repair itself. The sooner you stop smoking, the less damage you will do to your body.

Special Health Risks for Women

Smoking is dangerous for everybody, but there are special health risks for women.

More and more girls ages fourteen to seventeen are smoking more and more even in spite of these health risks. That might be due to cigarette advertising. It may also be because they think that cigarettes help keep their weight down. This is not true, however.

Smoking may make people feel less hungry or provide something to do besides snack. But smoking hurts your health. There are many other ways to keep your weight down and stay fit and healthy. Sports and exercise are fun ways to spend time with friends, and these activities keep your body strong, healthy, and looking and feeling great.

Lung cancer has replaced breast cancer as the leading killer disease of women. If you smoke and take birth control pills, you are ten times more likely to have a heart attack or stroke. Smoking increases the risk of heart attack for young women more than any other factor. You do not have to be old to have a heart attack.

Remember the warning label: "Smoking by pregnant women may result in fetal injury, premature birth, and low birth weight."

Why should you worry about that now? It may not seem important to you yet, but once you start smoking, it is very, very hard to quit. When you become a mother, you may still be smoking.

Babies of mothers who smoke have twice the risk of sudden infant death syndrome (SIDS). This disease kills babies suddenly in their sleep. Also, the babies of smokers have twice as many lung illnesses, such as bronchitis and pneumonia.

The Health Risks of Smoking: A Reminder

The earlier you start smoking, the earlier you can die from it.

- Cigarettes contain nicotine, tars, carbon monoxide, and other chemicals. Nicotine is a habit-forming drug. Tars coat your lungs and make it difficult to breathe. Carbon monoxide is deadly for your heart.

- Smoking causes lung diseases such as chronic bronchitis, emphysema, and lung cancer.

- Smoking causes heart disease, strokes, and heart attacks.

A baby's health can be affected if his or her mother smokes.

- The sooner you stop smoking, the less damage you will do to your body. The longer you smoke, the higher your chances of getting lung or heart diseases.

- There are special health risks for women who smoke. Lung cancer has replaced breast cancer as the leading type of cancer death among women.

- Women who smoke during pregnancy endanger their unborn babies.

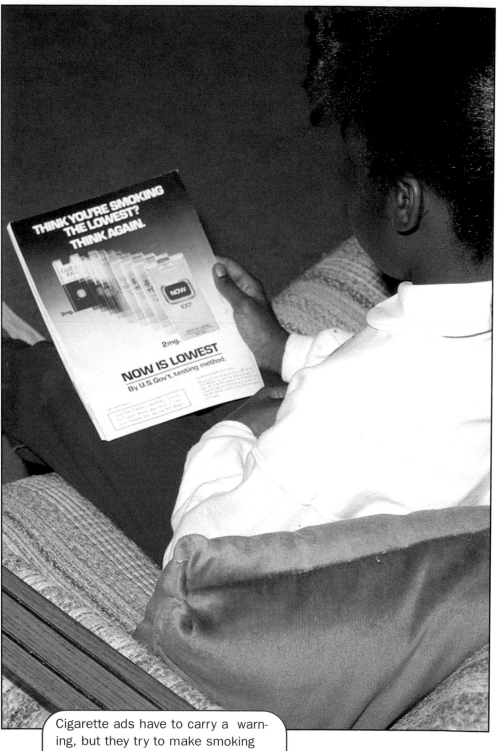

Cigarette ads have to carry a warning, but they try to make smoking look safe and glamorous.

Chapter Three

What You See Is Not What You Get

Cigarette advertisers have a hard job to do. Ads must make smoking look like something you will enjoy. They must make smoking look good enough to make you try it, even though the same ad has a warning about smoking being harmful. The ads must carry the warning because that is the law. This law was passed so that everyone would know the dangers of smoking.

Older people who smoke do not need advertising to convince them. A lot of people who smoke would stop if they could, but they are hooked. Smoking is a habit. Many people become addicted to the nicotine in tobacco. Their bodies need it, and they feel sick or nervous if they do not smoke.

Adults who do not smoke will probably not be convinced by ads that smoking is a good thing. At their age, they probably know the truth. However, tobacco companies and advertising executives target young people with ads that make smoking look cool.

Cigarette ads make it look as if you will have fun because you smoke. They make you think that smoking will make you popular. That kind of advertising suggestion is called association. Linking something pleasant with a particular product makes people want to try that product.

Often the ads show couples outdoors together or people playing sports. In real life, people who smoke a lot can have trouble breathing. Smoking makes it hard to play active sports. If you are on a team, the coach will tell you not to smoke.

Cigarette ads show people who are healthy, with glowing skin and brilliant white teeth. In truth, smoking stains your teeth. It makes your skin dull, and it makes your hair smell bad.

Some people think that cigarette advertising should not be allowed. It is not allowed on television. In New York City, cigarette advertising is no longer allowed on buses or subways.

Although it is against the law to sell cigarettes to minors (people younger than eighteen), cigarette ads seem to be directed toward younger and younger kids. One cigarette company uses a cartoon character in its ads.

Sometimes the character is shown with a group of other "cool" characters. These ads appear on billboards and in store windows. They also appear in magazines that kids read. One study showed that most fourth graders could more easily identify this cartoon character than a photo of the current president of the United States.

Cigarette makers would never publicly reveal the hazards of cigarette smoking, or they would lose huge amounts of money. Recently they have been sued in several states for not being truthful about the health risks. In March 1999, a jury in Oregon ordered tobacco company Philip Morris to pay $81 million to the family of a man who smoked Marlboro cigarettes for forty years before he died. In July 1999, a Florida jury ruled that cigarettes caused lung cancer and other diseases and that the makers intended to keep the dangers hidden from the public. Lawsuits against tobacco companies are increasing across the country.

A Different Kind of Advertising

There is another side to more recent cigarette advertising. Health-related groups like the American Cancer Society and the American Heart Association have ads, too. Their ads stress the dangers of smoking.

The message about the dangers of smoking is very important. The cigarette companies spend over a billion dollars a year to convince people that smoking is not bad for them. Now there is something being done to let people know the truth about smoking.

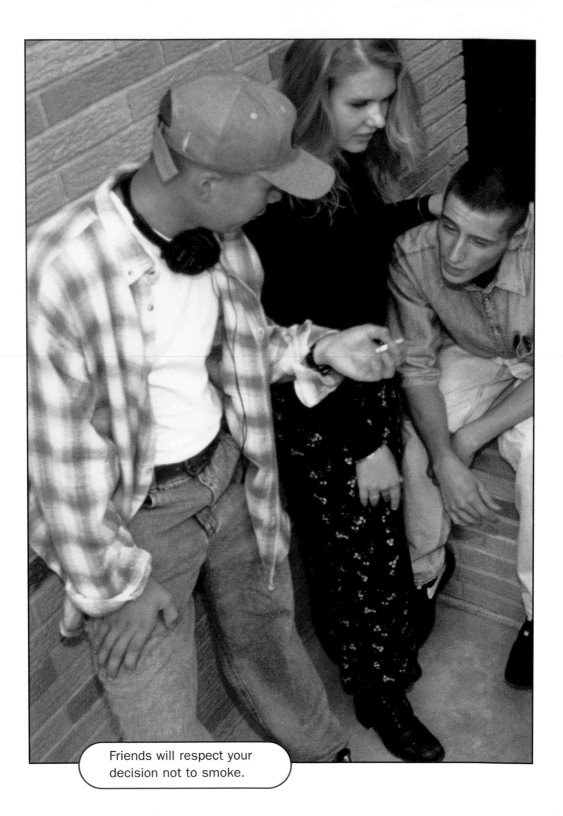

Friends will respect your decision not to smoke.

Chapter Four

It Is Your Choice

It is up to us, as individuals, to make our own decisions. We decide for ourselves what to do with our lives and with our bodies. That includes deciding what goes into our bodies.

It is important for us to make these choices, not to let others make them for us. If a friend offers you a cigarette, think before you accept it. Think carefully about everything you have learned about smoking. Are you ready to start a habit that will put your health permanently at risk?

If not, there are ways to say no without offending your friends. If they are truly your friends, they will respect your decision. This is how the situation might go:

After school Ryan is studying in the park with Logan, Danielle, and Gabe. Gabe pulls out a pack of cigarettes.

Gabe: Boy, do I need a smoke.

Logan: Let me bum a cigarette from you Gabe. Pass me that lighter.

Danielle: Me too! How about you Ryan?

Ryan: No, thanks. I'm not really into smoking.

Logan: You're not? How come? It's cool. Besides, you might like it. Gabe, pass over another cigarette.

Ryan: That's all right. I don't want one.

Gabe: What's the matter? Are you afraid? Try it. What's one tiny cigarette gonna do? It's not gonna kill you.

Ryan: I'm not afraid. I just don't think it's worth the risk. The thing is, it could kill me.

Danielle: It's no big deal if you just try one.

Ryan: Like I said, it's not worth the risk. My grandma died of emphysema from years of smoking, and I don't want that happening to me.

Gabe: Yeah, but how old was your grandma? I thought she lived a long life.

If someone offers you a cigarette at a party, you should not feel obligated to accept it.

Ryan: She was in her seventies, but she started smoking when she was my age. By the time she got sick, she was way too addicted to consider quitting, even when the doctor told her she had to. Before she died, she made me promise not to take up smoking. I'll never forget it.

Logan: Well, whatever, man. It's up to you.

Despite pressure from friends, Ryan stayed calm and said no to smoking. He remembered what smoking did to his grandmother and thus avoided a harmful life-long habit. Do not let peer pressure by your friends convince you to smoke. It might seem cool at first to smoke with friends because it makes you feel part of the group. However, it is your own health that is important. If you feel pressured by others, stand your ground. Trust your own beliefs. Your true friends will respect your decision if you choose not to smoke, and you will feel better about yourself in the long run.

Chapter Five

Smoking Is Drug Addiction

Every day we hear about the horrors of drug addiction. We read in the news about people overdosing on heroin or killing somebody to get money for crack. These are extreme cases of addiction, and most of us would not put smoking in the same category.

Like alcohol, nicotine is a legal drug. That does not make it any less of a drug, however. It may not have the immediate drastic effects of heroin or crack, but like those drugs, it is addictive. Smokers crave nicotine. They continue to smoke even though they know that it is harming them, and they often go through withdrawal and relapse after quitting. These things characterize drug addiction.

When the nicotine level in the bloodstream gets low, the body signals the mind: "Smoke a cigarette. I need nicotine."

Once you start smoking, it can be difficult to quit.

As soon as the smoker lights up, the nicotine is drawn into the lungs. It is quickly absorbed into the blood. The body's nicotine craving is satisfied—for a while.

Nicotine is a sneaky drug. When you first start smoking, you will find that it gives you a little burst of energy. That is the nicotine speeding up your heart.

After a while, you will notice that you feel tired between cigarettes. That happens when the nicotine level gets low. The tired feeling is your body's way of telling you that it wants nicotine.

The smoker is like a prisoner on a seesaw. When you are "down" on the seesaw, your body feels withdrawal. That is what makes you feel tired and sluggish. Your body wants its dose of nicotine.

As you smoke a cigarette, you go "up" on the seesaw. Nicotine speeds up the heart, and it gives you a rush. It stimulates the adrenal gland. That is the gland that makes adrenaline, the stuff that pumps through your veins when you are excited or nervous.

The nicotine gives you a rush, but when its level goes down, you feel the withdrawal symptoms. So although some people smoke to wake themselves up, they end up being more tired.

Nicotine Addiction: The Facts

◆ When you smoke, your body becomes addicted to nicotine.

31

Smoking can give you a quick spurt of energy, but it does not last long.

- ◆ It is very easy to become addicted to nicotine.
- ◆ Nicotine addiction makes you feel like a prisoner on a seesaw.

Chapter Six

Smoking: A Hard Habit to Break

The main reason it is so difficult to quit smoking is that you become addicted to nicotine. In addition to nicotine addiction, several other factors make quitting a challenge. For one thing, smoking is a habit. Habits are hard to break. You may also feel that smoking helps keep your weight down or ease your stress. Any one of these reasons can make quitting difficult.

Let's look at why a few teens say they would have a difficult time giving up smoking.

Kate: A Link Between Smoking and Weight Loss?

Kate: "I was pretty chubby when I started fig-ure skating five years ago. I was the heaviest girl in my skating group. Right about that time, I started smoking with my friends and started to lose weight. I don't know if smoking helped me lose weight or not, but it seemed like a strange coincidence to me. Smoking always messes me up, though, because I have to stop skating to cough. My boyfriend is always complaining that I have bad breath, and I've also noticed that my teeth are not really white anymore. But I'm afraid to give up smoking because I have heard that people start to gain weight as soon as they quit. I can't be fat if I'm going to be a figure skater."

Kate believes that smoking keeps her thin. On the other hand, she realizes that smoking will cause problems with her lungs, making it harder for her to have the strength to continue to skate. Kate should consider quitting smoking and starting a regular diet and exercise plan to supplement her skating regimen. She will feel better about herself knowing that she can maintain her proper body weight without smoking. Also, she will not suffer any of smoking's harmful side effects. An hour on the ice rink with her friends can give Kate an even better rush than from a cigarette.

Nell: Smoking and Responsibility

Nell: "Believe it or not, when I light up a cigarette, most of the time I don't even realize that

I've done it. Recently I almost got fired from a really good baby-sitting job because of my cigarette habit. One day the mother came home early, and I was holding the baby in one arm and a cigarette in the other hand. She was angry that I was smoking around her baby and exposing her to secondhand smoke. I promised never to do it again. Now I light up after I'm finished baby-sitting. Sometimes it's really hard to go a couple of hours without smoking. I wish I had never started smoking."

Nell's story illustrates how smoking becomes an unconscious habit. Have you ever tried to break a habit? Perhaps you crack your knuckles, twirl your hair, or bite your fingernails. Someone might have pointed it out to you, and you didn't realize that you were even doing it. Try quitting one of your habits for just one day. It's hard, isn't it?

Some people's smoking habits are linked directly to other habits. They might automatically light up a cigarette whenever they finish a meal, go to a party, or talk on the phone. When trying to kick the habit, it is important to identify when you smoke and to find something else to do with your hands and mouth during those times. Chewing gum or drinking a glass of cold water are two suggestions that might help you through this.

Vic: Smoking and Self-Esteem

Vic: "I'm kind of quiet and shy around groups of people. Smoking helps ease my anxiety, especially when I am with a group of people I don't know very well. Sometimes I'm the only one in the group who is smoking, and that makes me feel self-conscious, too. I just don't know what to do! Smoking helps me relax when I hang out with friends, but some people don't want to hang out with a smoker."

Vic uses smoking to lessen his shyness. However, instead of facing his anxiety about meeting new people, Vic hides his fears behind cigarettes. He has not looked inside of himself to find the cause of his shyness. Vic should think about why he is uncomfortable in groups of people. Maybe he needs to speak up more. Also, maybe he can bring along someone he knows so that he is not among strangers. Vic needs to take steps to overcome his shyness instead of hiding behind cigarettes.

Bobby: Can Smoking Cure the Blues?

Bobby: "I started smoking when my parents were getting divorced. They used to yell at each other all the time, and that made me nervous. I started smoking to calm down. Cigarettes really got me through the tough times when things weren't going right for me. Now I smoke to stay calm and in control. Smoking gives me the boost I need."

Bobby is experiencing the sadness and anxiety brought on by his parents' fighting and stress. He seeks comfort in cigarettes because they ease the pain for him. However, Bobby should talk to someone about his problems, such as a teacher, counselor, friend, or doctor. These people can offer support and helpful advice better than a pack of cigarettes can—without being hazardous to Bobby's health.

Many people smoke to relieve the normal stress of everyday life. This may seem like a good reason to smoke. However, if you can look ahead to your future, you might see that the stresses of lung cancer and heart problems are probably worse than anything you will encounter in your day-to-day life right now. Instead of smoking, try the following:

- Relaxing with a good book
- Exercising
- Taking a nap
- Walking or jogging

Exercise is one effective way to relieve stress.

- Watching your favorite movie
- Soaking in a bubble bath
- Having dinner with a good friend

If you anticipate a stressful situation coming up, such as a test or a big game, plan ahead and make extra time for your healthy stress busters. Do not try to relieve your stress with something that will only cause you harm.

Reasons Behind Smoking: A Roundup

- Smoking becomes a habit, and habits are hard to break.

- Smoking is not a healthy way to keep your weight down. Exercise and a good diet will help you manage your weight and keep you healthy.

- You might smoke without even thinking about it. There are certain situations in which people often smoke. For example, studying with your friends may be your signal to light up.

- Many people smoke in an attempt to calm their nerves and relieve stress. School, family, work, or exhaustion can cause stress. There are healthy ways to deal with stress, like napping, exercising, or talking with friends. Smoking should not be one of them.

Sports and smoking do not mix. Most smokers do not have enough energy to enjoy exercise.

Chapter Seven | Good Reasons Not to Smoke

You may have heard this expression before: "Kissing a smoker is like licking an ashtray." Smoker's breath has also been called zoo breath. Not only does a smoker's breath stink, but so do a smoker's hair and clothing. Smoking leaves brown or yellow marks on teeth and fingers as well.

You might start smoking to fit in with a certain group. How about being friends with people who do not smoke? Many nonsmokers think that smoking is disgusting. If you are a smoker, it could limit your social life.

Nonsmokers do not like the smell of smoke. They also do not like the fact that your cigarette smoke could hurt them. If you start smoking, you may actually lose more friends than you gain.

Today it is nearly impossible to smoke in public places. Many state and local governments as well as private companies have imposed bans on smoking in places such as offices, restaurants, and stadiums. Public awareness about secondhand smoke and the dangers it poses for nonsmokers have made the bans acceptable and widespread.

If you still are not convinced, perhaps you have not looked at the price of cigarettes lately. In New York City, for example, the average cost of a pack of cigarettes is around $3.60. If you smoke a pack a day at that amount, you will be spending about $1,314 a year. Certainly you can think of better things to do with that money.

Smoking also limits your senses of taste and smell. Studies have shown that smoking gives you wrinkles and bad breath, and it makes your skin look unhealthy.

Six Reasons Not to Smoke

- Smokers have stinky hair, breath, and clothes.

- Smoking can limit your social life. Nonsmokers do not want to be exposed to the health risks of smoking. Also, they do not like the stink of smoke. Nonsmokers may avoid smokers.

- Tough antismoking laws have made smoking illegal in public places such as offices, restaurants, and airplanes.

Bad breath is not romantic! Many smokers use gum or mints to cover up cigarette breath.

- ◆ Smoking is expensive.

- ◆ Smoking limits your senses of taste and smell.

- ◆ Smoking gives you wrinkles and makes your skin look unhealthy.

Nonsmokers are affected by the smoke around them.

Chapter Eight | **When Others Smoke**

Let's say that you do not smoke. Think about riding in a car or being in a closed room with a smoker. The smoker's burning cigarette makes it hard for you to breathe.

New studies have shown that the smoke from someone else's cigarette can be harmful to your health. That is one of the reasons why antismoking laws exist across the country. These laws were designed to help and protect nonsmokers.

So what are nonsmokers worried about?

Two kinds of smoke come from a lighted cigarette:

- Mainstream smoke
- Sidestream smoke, also called secondhand smoke

Mainstream smoke is what the smoker inhales into his or her lungs. Think of a smoker taking a drag in slow motion. The smoke passes through the filter of the cigarette. The filter traps some of the chemicals and tars. Then the smoke enters the lungs. The lungs filter out more of the harmful substances. Finally the smoker exhales.

Sidestream smoke is the smoke that goes directly into the air from the tip of a burning cigarette. This smoke does not pass through a filter. It contains a lot more carbon monoxide, tars, and nicotine than the mainstream smoke.

Sidestream smoke is what nonsmokers breathe when they are in a room with smokers. The carbon monoxide makes them feel tired and gives them headaches. Studies have shown that nonsmokers who live with smokers die younger than people who live in smoke-free houses.

A famous television writer died of lung cancer. He had never smoked, but his colleague had smoked more than two packs of cigarettes every day. The two men had worked together for over twenty years. How do you think the surviving coworker felt about what had happened? Would you want something like that to happen to somcone you care about?

What does all this mean? The nonsmoker who lives or works with smokers can get sick from the smoke just as smokers can. It that fair? What do you think?

The smoke from lit cigarettes in an ashtray can be harmful.

Secondhand Smoke: The Risks

- The smoke from a cigarette can harm non-smokers, too.

- Mainstream smoke is what a smoker inhales. It is filtered by the smoker's lungs. More poisonous to the nonsmoker is sidestream smoke, which contains all the unfiltered poisons: tars, carbon monoxide, and so on.

- The nonsmoker who lives or works with smokers can also get sick from smoke.

Talking with counselors and other teens can be helpful in making a decision about not smoking.

Chapter Nine | Do You WANT to Smoke? Make Your Own Decision

Now you know more about smoking. You know how it affects your body, your appearance, and your health. You know more about why people start and why it is hard to stop.

Maybe you have not started smoking, but you are thinking about it. Choosing whether or not to smoke is an important decision. The following test will help you. If you are already a smoker, try this test. It may change your mind about smoking.

This is the Smoker's Decision Test. It is not like a school test. There are no right or wrong answers. This is a way to help you get a clearer idea of what is important to you. It will help you make a decision about smoking.

Make a photocopy of this page. Do not write in the book itself.

Part One: Reasons for Smoking

	Very Important	Not Important
Smoking can make you feel like part of the group.	☐	☐
Smoking can make you feel more mature and glamorous.	☐	☐
If you already smoke, you would be giving up something that makes you feel good.	☐	☐
Smoking relaxes you.	☐	☐
You do not want to admit that it was a mistake to start smoking.	☐	☐
Quitting might cause you to gain weight.	☐	☐
You do not want to face the possibility that your smoking is out of control and you cannot quit.	☐	☐

Most people find it easy to use the result of this test. They can see clearly how they feel about smoking.

First, look closely at what you have checked in the Very Important column. Then proceed to part two.

Make a photocopy of this page. Do not write in the book itself.

Part Two: Reasons for Not Smoking

	Very Important	Not Important
Smoking can limit your social life.	☐	☐
Smoking is bad for your health. It can even kill you.	☐	☐
It is bad for the health of others around you.	☐	☐
Smoking has special health risks for women.	☐	☐
Most public places prohibit smoking.	☐	☐
It reduces athletic ability.	☐	☐
It is an expensive habit.	☐	☐
Smoking makes your breath, clothes, and hair smell bad.	☐	☐

Now write out your very important reasons for smoking and your very important reasons for not smoking. Compare them side by side.

Look at your reasons. Decide for yourself if you are going to start. If you have already started, decide if you are going to continue or quit. Either way, make your own decision.

Chapter Ten | Quit Smoking: Step by Step

If you are a smoker, you may have tried to quit. You may have found that it is very hard. However, nearly half of all living adults who ever smoked have quit. That is millions of people who have quit smoking. You can, too. There is no guaranteed method; you have to find what is right for you. Here are some steps to follow to help you kick the habit.

List Your Reasons to Quit Smoking

Make a list of all the reasons that you want to quit (i.e., "I hate the way cigarettes smell," "I want clean lungs"). You must decide why you want to quit smoking. Is it the cost? The complaints from your boyfriend or girlfriend?

Write down these reasons and keep the list with you. Every day, pull out the list and remind yourself: This is why I'm quitting.

Set a Date

Choose a quitting date on the calendar. Do not change it. If you know that you smoke most often at school or work, choose a weekend to quit. That will make the first one or two days easier.

Some people quit cold turkey. This means that they choose a day to quit, and then quit—completely.

Other people cut down first. That means that they smoke fewer cigarettes and then they quit.

Cutting Down

If you want to cut down on your smoking, first decide on a date to quit. Then begin to cut down gradually as you get closer to that date.

You also probably smoke some cigarettes without even thinking about it. Other cigarettes, like the ones you smoke after a meal or a test, are more important to you. At those times you really want a cigarette. The trick to cutting down is to decide which are important to you—and smoke only those cigarettes.

You can plan ahead of time. Carry the exact number of cigarettes you have decided to smoke that day. It might be just three or four.

Another way to cut down is to smoke only half a cigarette at a time or change to a brand of cigarettes you do not like.

Still another way is to delay having a cigarette when you want one. Instead of smoking when you want to, wait ten minutes. That way you can think it over and decide if you really want that cigarette. After ten minutes, you may not even want the cigarette anymore.

Change your smoking routine. Try keeping your cigarettes in a different place. Smoke with your other hand. Don't do anything else when smoking and think about how you feel while you are doing it.

Cutting down is great, but do not fool yourself. You may think that you have things under control and that you can quit anytime. That is not true. Most people who cut down soon return to their original number of cigarettes.

Set your quitting date!

Tell Everybody You Are Quitting

Tell your family and friends about your plan to quit smoking. That will make it harder for you to back out of it. It will also let others know that you might be cranky and a little hard to live with for a few days.

Do Not Change Your Eating Habits

Do not reach for a snack every time you want a cigarette. Chew gum. Exercise. If you snack, you might gain weight. People use weight gain as an excuse to start smoking again.

Reward Yourself

Find other things to do that are fun or make you happy. An easy choice is exercise. Exercise is good because you have to use your whole body. That reminds you of how important your lungs are. Also, exercise makes you feel good. Take up a hobby such as photography, music, or skateboarding. Go to the movies, the zoo, the beach, or a concert. To pay for these activities, use the money you are not spending on cigarettes!

Do Not Give Up—You Can Quit

If you smoke a cigarette or even an entire pack, do not feel that you have failed. Pull out your list and remind yourself why you want to quit. If your reasons have changed, make a new list. When you get the urge to smoke, do something else instead. Keep busy.

Watch for "smoke signals"—like a friend lighting up. Know that this is the time when you are most likely to smoke. Be strong and do not give in to smoking. It will pay off.

Chapter Eleven | Getting Help When You Want to Quit

As you have already learned, either from reading this book or through painful personal experience, it is very hard to quit smoking. You may believe that you cannot do it on your own and that you need help. Remember, do not be afraid to ask for help if you need it. Be proud of yourself for realizing your own limitations and understanding that you need help. Getting help is easy. Many organizations can help people like you overcome their smoking habit.

Check with your favorite teacher, guidance counselor, or school nurse to find out if your school offers a program to help students kick the habit. If your school does not have such a program, be the force behind starting one.

Three major organizations that are already in place and ready to help are the American Cancer Society, the American Lung Association, and the American Heart Association. All three have programs to help you stop smoking. For information on contacting these organizations, look in the Where to Go for Help section of this book.

Help can come in several forms. Your doctor can prescribe drugs to help break the addiction. Some people succeed in quitting smoking by using special chewing gum. Others find help by using a nicotine patch, which is a small pad (similar to a bandage) that, when placed on your body, releases nicotine into your skin. It gives your body the nicotine it craves without all the other harmful chemicals in a cigarette. Both the gum and the patch can help steer your body away from nicotine.

You may find it helpful to get some counseling. Deciding to quit smoking is a major step and can create feelings of stress, unhappiness, and irritability. You may have to cope with changing emotions in addition to coping with fighting your nicotine cravings. Sometimes it helps to have someone to talk to, who will listen to you and offer you the support you need to get through this.

Now you probably know much more about smoking. Do you still find smoking hip and glamorous? You have learned about the health risks associated with smoking as well as how smoking affects or influences your social life. If you are curious about smoking, get all the facts before you take that first cigarette, cigar, or pipe. If you are already addicted and you want to quit smoking, remember that there are people and organizations that can help you on the road to recovery. Only you can make this important life decision.

Glossary

addictive Causing a person's body to depend on a chemical.

adrenal gland A gland that produces the hormone adrenaline. Adrenaline prepares the body for emergency action; it makes the heart work harder.

bronchi Tubes in the lungs.

cancer A disease that causes cells to grow abnormally and become tumors. These tumors spread and interfere with normal cell growth.

carbon dioxide A gas that is breathed out of the body during exhalation.

carbon monoxide A gas that is poisonous. It is one of the chemicals in cigarette smoke.

chronic bronchitis A lung condition caused by smoking, marked by severe coughing and irritation of the lungs.

cilia Tiny hairs in the bronchi that clear away mucus.

craving A great desire or longing.

drag The inhalation of cigarette smoke.

emphysema A severe lung disease.

glamorous Full of excitement and romance.

heart disease This includes a number of diseases such as heart attack, stroke, hardening of the arteries, and blood clots.

influence To sway or affect.

lung cancer A disease in which the cells of the lungs divide uncontrollably. Smoking is a major cause of lung cancer.

mainstream smoke What the smoker inhales and exhales.

mucus A slippery secretion of the mucous membranes.

nicotine A drug found in tobacco smoke to which your body becomes addicted.

premature Early; before being fully ready.

secondhand/sidestream smoke The smoke that comes from the burning end of a cigarette.

stress Tension or pressure.

tar A sticky black substance found in tobacco. It coats the lungs when smoke is inhaled.

withdrawal The process of stopping the body's dependency on an addictive drug; physical and mental effects an addict suffers after ceasing to take an addictive drug.

Where to Go for Help

Organizations

American Cancer Society
19 West 56th Street
New York, NY 10019
(800) ACS-2345
Web site:
http://www.cancer.org

American Lung Association
1740 Broadway
New York, NY 10019
(212) 315-8700
Web site:
http://www.lungusa.org

Office on Smoking and Health
Centers for Disease Control
and Prevention
Mail Stop K-67
4770 Buford Highway NE
Atlanta, GA 30341

(770) 488-5705
(800) CDC-1311
Web site:
http://www.cdc.gov/tobacco

In Canada

Canadian Cancer Society
National Office
10 Elkhorn Avenue
Toronto, ON M4V 3B1
(416) 961-7223
Web site: http://www.cancer.ca

Canadian Lung Association
National Office
1900 City Park Drive, #508
Blair Business Park
Gloucester, ON K1J 1A3
(613) 747-6776
Web site: http://www.lung.ca

For Further Reading

DeAngelis, Gina. *Nicotine and Cigarettes*. New York: Chelsea House, 1999.

Fisher, Edwin B., Jr., Ph.D., and Toni L. Goldfarb. *American Lung Association: 7 Steps to a Smoke-Free Life*. New York: John Wiley and Sons, 1998.

Gebhardt, Jack. *Help Your Smoker Quit: A Radically Happy Strategy for Nonsmoking Parents, Kids, Spouses, and Friends*. Minneapolis, MN: Fairview Press, 1998.

Hyde, Margaret O. *Know About Smoking*. New York: Walker and Co., 1995.

Lang, Susan S., and Beth H. Marks. *Teens and Tobacco*. New York: Twenty-First Century Books, 1996.

Mayer, Gerald S., Ph.D. *When It Hurts Too Much To Quit: Smoking and Depression*. Phoenix, AZ: Desert City Press, 1997.

McMillan, Daniel. *Teen Smoking: Understanding the Risks*. Springfield, NJ: Enslow Publishers, 1997.

Pringle, Laurence. *Smoking*. New York: Morrow, 1996.

Wetherall, Charles F. *Quit for Teens: Read This Book and Stop Smoking*. Kansas City, MO: Andrews & McMeel Publishing, 1995.

Index

About the Author

Elizabeth Keyishian is an associate editor for an award-winning children's science magazine. In addition to writing for young adults, she has published humorous essays. A graduate of Wesleyan University, Ms. Keyishian lives in New York City.

About the Editor

Evan Stark is a well-known sociologist, educator, and therapist as well as a popular lecturer on women's and children's health issues. Dr. Stark was a Henry Rutgers Fellow at Rutgers University, an associate at the Institution for Social and Policy Studies at Yale University, and a Fulbright Fellow at the University of Essex. He is the author of many publications in the field of family relations and is the father of four children.

Acknowledgments and Photo Credits

Cover photo by Photo Researchers, Inc.; p. 11 © H. Armstrong Roberts, Inc.; p. 24 by Guillermina de Ferrari; pp. 27, 30 by Les Mills; p. 38 by Ira Fox; all other photos by Stuart Rabinowitz.

Layout Design

Michael J. Caroleo